The B2B Crossover

A Basketball Approach to Becoming an Entrepreneur and Living the Dream

By Craig Levine

Table of Contents

Authors Note:

Thank you for purchasing a copy of Basketball to Business Crossover. This book outlines starting a company in a familiar way, through basketball. One reason the B2B crossover works so well in forming in a business is that basketball itself is one of the newest big business. In 2016 the salary cap increased 25% due to very large profits establishing the sport as a formidable corporation. Let's not forget the advertisements that will be installed on NBA jerseys next year.

In writing this book my goal is to give you confidence to start your own business. To give you confidence in me, I'm fresh off of MBA classes including Lean Startup, Six Sigma, and of course I bring my own entrepreneurial experiences from time to time. You'll notice many basketball fundamentals that any basketball player knows by heart like the pivot and court vision. Any fan of the NBA will be entertained by the business decisions players face when entering free agency and much more.

Enjoy this book with it's rare and possible ahead of it's time… parallel from Basketball to Business.

Chapter 1

Court Vision

- "You've got to have the vision to see an opportunity."

So you think you've got what it takes to enter the NBA of business. Starting your own business, being your own boss and controlling how much money you want to make. Now to be honest this isn't a get rich quick guide, you'll have the put in the work. That means your life is and will be your company. Are you up for the challenge? Can you handle the heat? We are going to find out whether you've got the fortitude to succeed at the highest level of your young career.

I'm keeping this book interesting to you by sharing both lean startup knowledge and how closely it relates to the great game of basketball. Besides the obvious fact that I'm hoping to make some money on this book (share with your friends :D), I realized how much good this book could do for people with little business savvy. In fact if you follow this guide, you'll be a qualified entrepreneur with ideas to kickstart a company. Now are you ready to start a company.

How many times can you remember watching a teammate dribbling around and after all this dribbling he throws up some fade away garbage shot? You and your teammates are making cuts, setting screens and rolling to the basket. Meanwhile, this guy passes on all these opportunities to satisfy himself and not what's best to score.

Having a vision for starting a business is paramount to seeing success. The business is what you will be putting your time and resources into for the next few years. It would be best not to sink all of your time and money into something that customers don't want to buy, and you don't even have an interest in. Look around and see what sells the most for a start.

The B2B Crossover: being open to new opportunities is crucial to success. What the ball handler who only wants to score, didn't see was teammates missed for an easy layup opportunity, and now value has diminished along with respect. In business, spotting the next trend and opportunity are very important for being part of the next wave or being left behind.

Nobody knows about court vision more than a point guard. When he gets past half court, it's up to him to make a play happen and control the offense. It's up to him to weigh his options and make the right play, and it is up to him to Not Turn The Ball Over. Let me emphasize that in case you didn't just hear a coach yelling your head off about that turnover that led to a breakaway 2 handed slam, DO NOT TURN THE BALL OVER.

They say that every true success in business happens only after a person has experienced failure. Even then 50% of the businesses fail after five years. Why do startups fail you may ask and here are four reasons, cofounders fight, can't build the product, nobody funds the idea, and the market wasn't analyzed.

The B2B Crossover: have more success than failures, even Chris Paul and Pistol Pete turned the ball over, the difference between them and you is how they took it in stride, reacting quickly and making the play at the next chance they got.

Big men have a vision too. I've seen some amazing passes to slashers to the rim and even a few reverse alley-oops, big man to small man for a rim rocker. I'll never forget Yao Ming in one of his first all-star games still getting a feel for the NBA, passing a behind-the-back pass to Steve Francis for the windmill alley-oop. Though assists happen, big men, without a doubt, have a different vision. Their objective is to make a move and score more times than not.

Big companies are entitled to brand recognition and initial investment from either bankers or private equity. Most filed as a corporation; they have strict rules and regulations that make a hierarchy of talent that requires anything from sales, marketing, engineering, management, human resources, etc. Moreover, of course, the board of directors is at the top. Your company should start with either an LLC or sole proprietorship, and work its way up. You never know, your business could rise to become a corporation one day.

The B2B Crossover: Just like in basketball every member of a team has a role, it's up to those team members to define their part, and master their trade. Although it would seem natural for the Centers of every team to be the best players, rarely is that the case, especially with the small-ball Golden State Warriors and the LeBron-led Cavaliers leading the evolution of basketball. Same goes in business, the best entrepreneurs who have passion and love for what they do become the most successful and make the most money.

Business Analytics:

2015 filings for companies

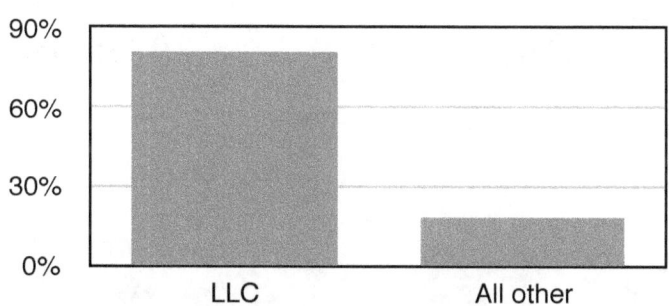

Percentage of Company Success Rates

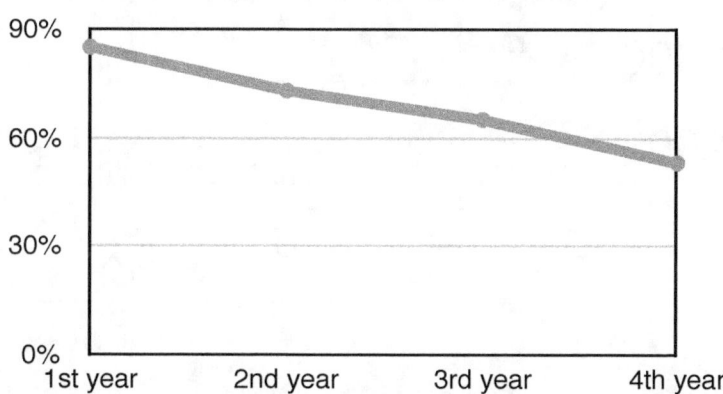

*Success rate is based on number of companies recognized and in good paper-work standing by each state

Basketball Statistics:

Jason Kidd 1994-1995 to 2012-2013

Career Assist to Turnover Ratio: **3.0**

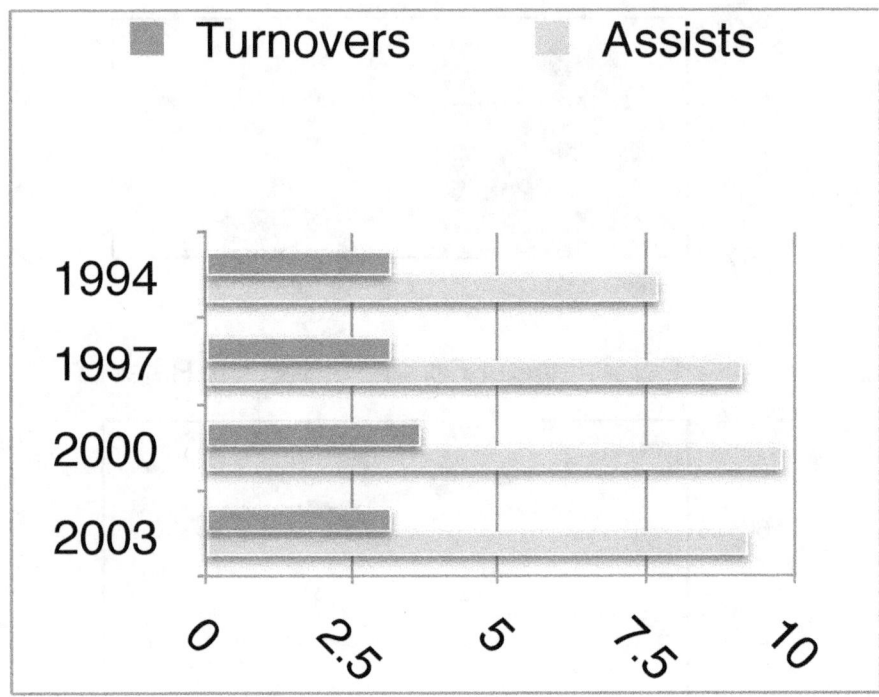

Challenge

Search for a Business Models and Check in the checkbox for one or more industries that interest you. Note if the industry is not under here check other.

- ☐ Food and Beverage/ Restaurant
- ☐ Religious Organization
- ☐ Software/Mobile Application
- ☐ IT Consulting
- ☐ Fantasy Sports Services
- ☐ Supply Chain/ Logistics
- ☐ Fitness and Wellness
- ☐ Services
- ☐ Education
- ☐ Retail and Online Store
- ☐ Real Estate
- ☐ Farm and Food Production
- ☐ Bar and Nightlife
- ☐ Construction and Engineering
- ☐ Doctor/Dentist/Physical Therapy
- ☐ Other _____

Challenge

Write down your five best startup ideas and then rank them from highest probability of happening vs. this idea should not be a business. Five Stars for your best idea.

☆☆☆☆☆ 1) _____

_____

_____

☆☆☆☆☆ 2) _____

_____

_____

☆☆☆☆☆ 3) _____

_____

_____

☆☆☆☆☆ 4) _____

_____

☆☆☆☆☆ 5) _____

_____

_____

Chapter 2

The Pivot

- "When you pick up the ball, use the pivot to your advantage. Pivot too late and you'll be trapped."

Anytime you've been in the post against a big man, he will be preventing you from getting a clean shot. You've got to find a way to get the 2 points or get to the free throw line. In the spot you've got a few options go left, go right, back him down or shoot over the top. Either way you go, you will need one of the most strategically important moves in basketball, the Pivot. Often coupled with the pump fake it will make a big man look like a fool.

Entrepreneur classes have taught me that the Pivot is a very advanced tactic that takes the business a step toward a different direction. It is true and here is an example, after six months of selling an artificially flavored juice, sales were decreasing as customers began complaining of stomach aches after drinking it. The company then pivoted to replace the artificial flavoring with natural ingredients to appease the customers and stay in business. This pivot saved the company.

The B2B Crossover: with a basketball in the post, a pivot can mean the difference between scoring and getting a shot blocked. These moves are remarkably applicable to business where the stakes may be getting new cash flow or losing the company altogether.

Another type of pivot is from the top of the key in a triple threat. After weighing options in both directions, you'll see a guard or forward take their first step toward the basket. This first step needs to be quick to get past the first line of defense.

In your position as a prospective businessman, you could find it nerve-wracking to go up against companies with established products and brand name. We will discuss ways to compete against them and how to create your own market altogether.

The B2B Crossover: be willing to take the first leap into starting your business with confidence and speed, just as you'd drive to the rim with that first move toward the goal.

Avoiding traps is tough but getting out of a trap is twice as hard. If you have ever picked up your dribble, you may have only one or two pivots before a decision must be made. Not to mention the 5-second rule to force a turnover. One move and a second move is all the time you have before a decision must be made to get the ball out of there.

A trap in business can take multiple forms. The most clear one is a legal infringement: trademark, copyright, and patents can all result in the disbandment of your company. A sole proprietorship or partnership could lead to your house or car being used as collateral forcing you into bankruptcy. This is the worst business situation, PREVENT this by filing as an LLC to avoid such action. Your first move out of the trap is to see it coming ahead of time, get your own trademark or copyright at LegalZoom for about $400. They focus on, search and take care of everything while you just register your logo or catch phrase slogan. Patents usually cost $3,000 to $25,000 depending on how expansive the design or use of it is.

The B2B Crossover: Know the potential traps that opponents will lay out whether they are competitive businesses or rival teams. Also know that when you get into the trap how hard it will be to get yourself out. The best thing to do is to think ahead, perform searches at USPTO or the many websites that can take that action. You don't want to end up bankrupt or siting on the bench.

Business Analytics:

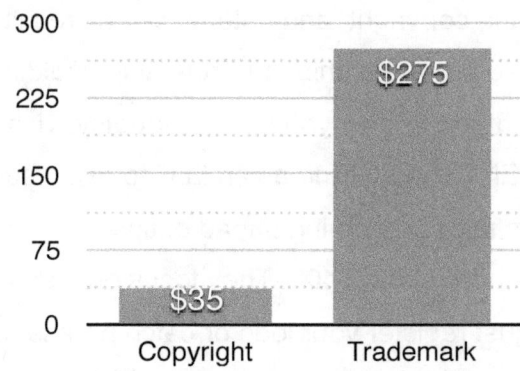

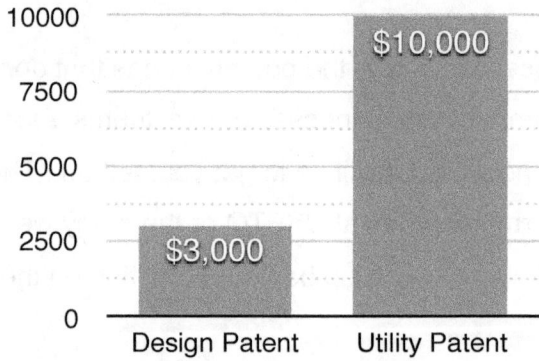

*Prices are averages, your price quote may differ.

Basketball Statistics:

Kareem Abdul-Jabbar was one of the all-time greats. If you ever watched him play, you'd know how fantastic his hook shot was. Not only that but he knew how to pivot to advance his game. Check out how his stats below and watch his great plays online.

Career MPG	36.8
Career PPG	24.6
Career RPG	11.2
Career BPG	2.6
Seasons	20

Hakeem Olajuwon invented the Dream Shake. The Dream Shake was the greatest use of pivots of all time. Never before has a seven footer been as quick with his moves as Hakeem and he remains a top 5 center of all time without dispute. Check out his Dream Shake online.

Career MPG	36.4
Career PPG	22.5
Career RPG	11.4
Career BPG	3.2
Seasons	17

Challenge

Pivot your company to become something different in the same industry or to take a leap in a new industry altogether. Every time you pivot, it should formulate a better product or service for the consumer.

Original Idea: _____

_____

_____

Pivot within same industry: ex. Vitamin Water

_____

_____

Why is this a better product or idea? _____

_____

_____

Pivot into a different industry: ex. Netflix*

_____

_____

Why is this industry better? _____

_____

_____

*Netflix began as a DVD business but pivoted to a subscription service completely online

*Vitamin Water pivoted their marketing to include a more revitalizing feel with more health benefits

Challenge

How you file your company and checking for trademarks/copyrights may seem a trivial task. However, I can ensure you that it is not, there are lawyers paid to hunt down infringements.

Name of company: _____

_____

Does it infringe on any company with the same name in the same industry?

_____

_____

How will you file your company? LLC? Sole Proprietorship? Corporation?

_____

_____

Write down a few slogans you might like to for your company.

_____

_____

_____

Now search for the trademark via USPTO or trademark search website. Infringement laws that if the slogan is close enough in sound or lettering, a lawsuit is possible. If Yes (Cannot use) If No (Can use)

Chapter 3

Big City Market vs. Fan Base Market

- "Are you selling a product your hometown wants, or the nation needs?"

When LeBron James left Cleveland to go to big city Miami, he showed everyone the difference between playing for loyal fans and playing for a big city with loads of talent. Both options would have given him a max contract so the money wouldn't change up front. However, the endorsements would skyrocket by going to Miami and winning championship rings with the big 3 (Lebron, Bosh and Wade).

As an entrepreneur, you will have to decide how you will market your product or software application. Will you market the product as something the entire world will want to buy such as an iPhone app, household item or car accessory? Or will you sell it to a specific local market such as a hydration backpack for 18 - 24-year-old male college students on spring break at the local music festival?

The B2B Crossover: The more specific your market then the higher your fan base loyalty will become. Whereas the more people that can be reached then the higher the potential to grow.

Players that stayed with their team developed such a loyal fan base that their careers benefitted from it. The home court advantage translated to more wins. John Stockton and Karl Malone were a dynamic duo to be reckoned with any opposing team playing in Utah. Although they were never able to win a ring, they made the playoffs in all of their 18 years together! This is an amazing stat in itself. Coupled with the fact that only 3 million people live in Utah say one thing - those 3 million people loved Stockton and Malone. The loyalty from their fans meant more to these players than leaving town for a big name city like Los Angeles or New York.

There are certainly perks to going after a specific market rather than the entire world. For instance, communication between you and your specific market is better. Customers are more accessible for interviews and validation. What this means is you will know your customers connection to your product before you sell it to the entire market on a large scale.

The B2B Crossover: Loyalty has many perks that enable you to validate your idea to become a business. Selling Christmas trees from your backyard for instance, enables you to develop customer relationships. Generate enough sales of your trees and soon you will be running a Christmas tree farm for your entire community. Stockton and Malone turned the Utah Jazz into a Western Conference force for 18 straight years. Not winning the ring must have been a disappointment. However, they have the respect Utah fans for their entire lives.

Free agents that bounce around the league typically have a tendency to play wherever a team needs them to attain a ring or more money. Such players like Drew Gooden have much to offer teams and likely will have a longer career because they can bring their game to any team throughout the country (and Toronto).

Some businesses tend to bring a specific value to a city or region and then move to other cities or regions once they have saturated the market. This area of economics is called regional economic performance, and it can impact a company's decision to move to a different state or country.

The B2B Crossover: The first time I ever had a Dunkin' Donuts was in Boston, Massachusetts. They have more sweets and cream in that thing then a sugar mama. The franchise expanded through the years, and now I have it time-to-time where I live (#Fearthebeard). The point is simply this; sometimes the region becomes saturated, and either you grow to other places or pack up and move altogether.

Business Analytics:

The two pie graphs show increasingly specific target markets. Note of all the males in the US, only 4% are in the target market.

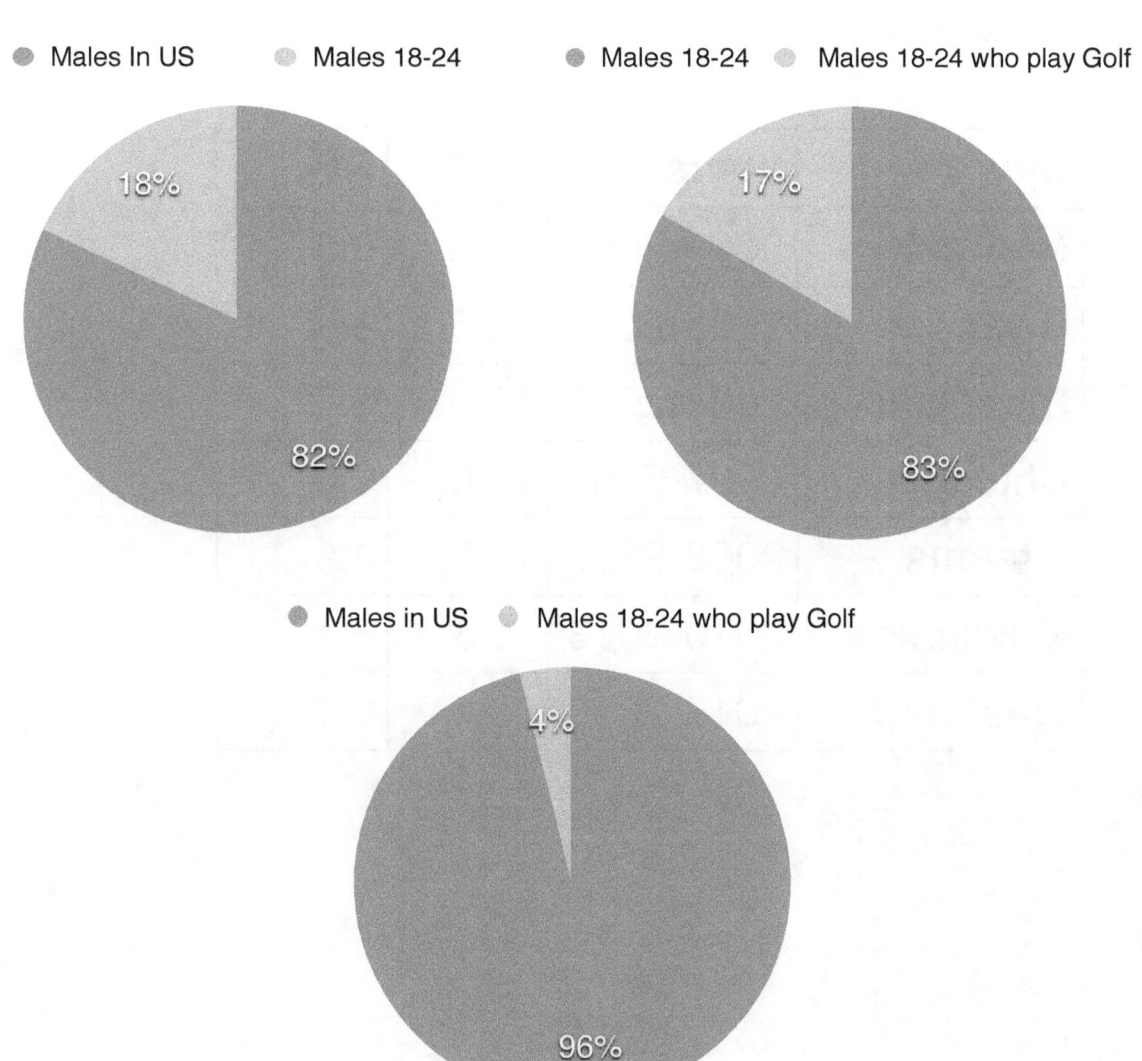

Basketball Statistics:

Free agents that bounce around the league are role players or contributors of some kind. **Drew Gooden** is a fine example, below are his stats of all the teams he has played for:

City	Years	PPG	RPG
Memphis	2002-2003	12.5	6.5
Orlando	2003-2004	13.6	8.4
Cleveland	2004-2007	12.0	8.7
Chicago	2007-2008	12.0	6.0
5 teams	2008-2010	11.5	4.9
Milwaukee	2010-2013	11.3	6.1
Washington	2013-2016	6.2	3.2

Challenge

When you create a company, you can almost feel the difference whether your marketing for the world or marketing for your community. Outline the path you want to choose below.

Maximum Potential Market: _____

_____

Targeted Age Group: _____

_____

More Male or Female customers: _____

_____

Where will customers be using the product?: _____

_____

_____

Will there be more demand locally or nationally?: _____

_____

_____

Can you scale it to be international? _____

_____

_____

_____

Challenge

How will you market this company locally or nationally? Check all that apply.

For Local City or Community

- ☐ Word of mouth
- ☐ Local Fliers, Business Cards
- ☐ Launch Party
- ☐ Promotions
- ☐ Coupons
- ☐ Local Newspaper, TV or Radio Ads
- ☐ Other _____

_____

For Nationally

- ☐ Facebook/Instagram Ads
- ☐ Google Ads
- ☐ Vine
- ☐ National TV Ads
- ☐ GroupOn/Reddit/Pinterest
- ☐ Other _____

_____

Chapter 4

MVP

- "You gotta build a product that people are going to want, put emotion into it, let's build an MVP."

Can you name the greatest NBA players of all time? If you answered LeBron James, Michael Jordan and Kobe Bryant you'd probably be close. Now answer this. Why are they entitled to this honor and got lucky? Did they just have the drive to become the greatest of all time? Either way, they worked hard and put in the effort both on and off the court. They lived and breathed the game. They had to continue to develop their game from college to rookie year, and beyond.

So you've decided to be an entrepreneur and the ball is in your court. Let me ask you something, how are you going to get a product or software to the market? By Magic? Something like that. I was thinking a 3 step process. The first step is identifying the problem that you will be fixing with this product. The second step is answering what does your product do to relieve the customer of pain from this problem. And the final step is building an MVP or <u>minimal viable product</u>.

The B2B Crossover: just like the best NBA players, you've got to earn everything and follow the steps to success. The MVP is a great way to get there and ensures a big leap towards for getting your product to market.

Breaking down a jump shot in practice can have short and long-term benefits. Improved accuracy, a stronger guide hand, and better ball rotation are just 3 of the benefits. Take notice of how many shots Kyle Korver or the superstar Steph Curry take in practice. These guys are phenomenal in the games, and it stems from that consistent work they put in on the practice courts.

In the business world you may think of making a product just as many famous entrepreneurs have, in their own garage. Steve Jobs and Steve Wozniak of Apple developed their first computers in Steve Job's garage. Work with the resources that you have and make it happen whether it be a creative straw to drink out of, or solar powered panels to keep streets lit at night.

The B2B Crossover: The best shooters in the world and the best entrepreneurs in the world have something in common. They know what they are good at, and they know what they have to work with. That doesn't mean they don't have a crazy amount of determination. Rather these guys know what they are doing to reach their goals.

Challenge

This challenge is your MVP or minimal viable product. The product should have the features that relieve a customer's pain. A good example would be making a doughnut MVP, a plain doughnut. One day you will be making the glazed variety with sprinkles, but for now it's just a plain doughnut to alleviate a customers hunger.

Product: _____
_____

Minimum Features: _____
_____
_____
_____

Pain alleviated: _____
_____
_____
_____

How is it a better solution to the problem? _____
_____
_____
_____

Challenge

How much will it cost to build a prototype of this product and how much do you foresee that it will cost when you mass produce the product. Give approximate costs. Chapter 6 goes into this subject further.

Expenses	Product Prototype	Mass Produced Product
Research and Development	Min $ Max $	Min $ Max $
Manufacturing	Min $ Max $	Min $ Max $
Packaging and Shipping	Min $ Max $	Min $ Max $

Business Analytics:

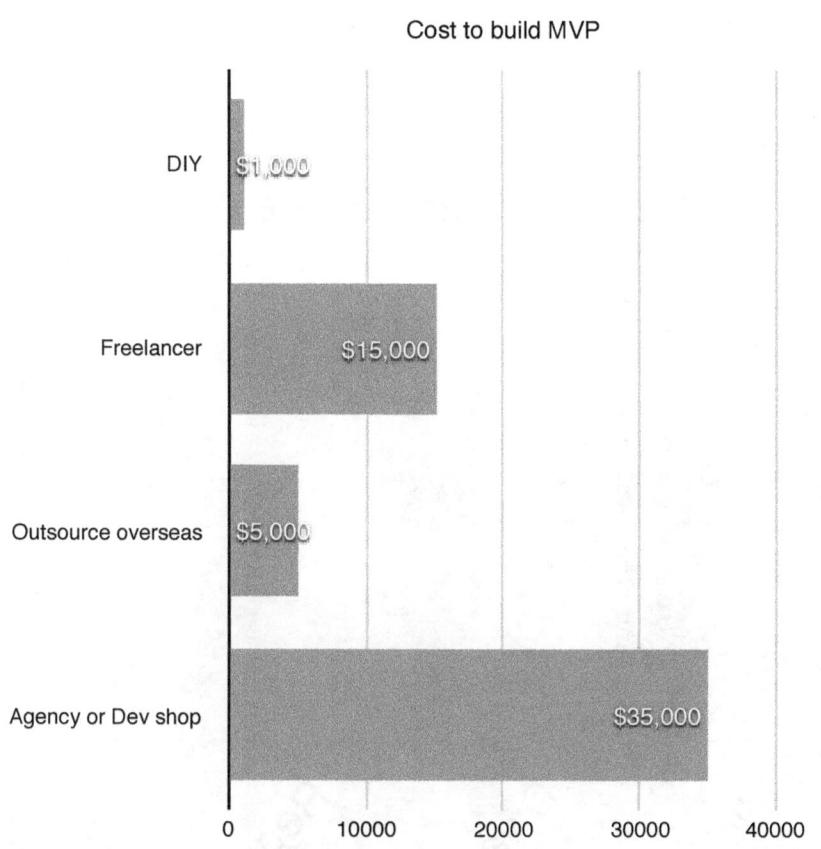

Cost to build MVP

*DIY is an acronym for Do It Yourself

Basketball Statistics:

Here are some of the best scorers in the game and their statistics in their very first NBA Game.

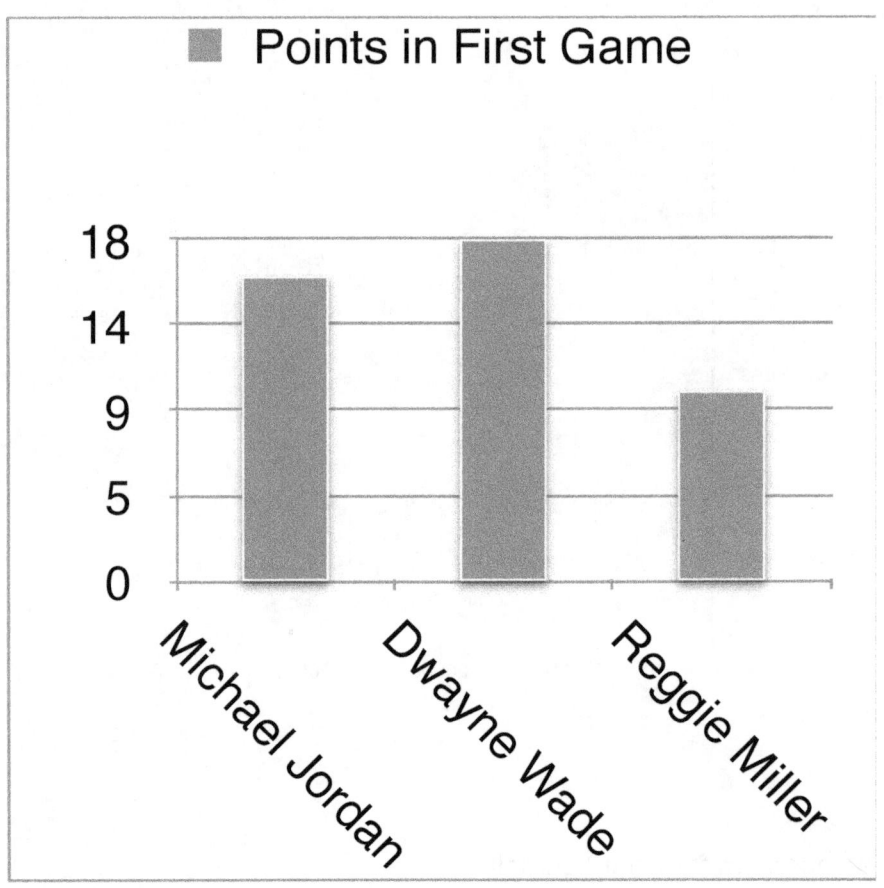

Chapter 5

Dream Team

- "Fantasy Draft your entrepreneurial dream team."

In this chapter, we will examine five different types of teams to demonstrate how you can run a business in different ways with different people. This chapter will be formatted differently so keep up.

The first team is the "One-Man-Show". This team has a superstar and a whole lotta role players whose fan admiration keeps the entrepreneurship alive. Without a doubt the greatest example of this kind of team is the 2001 Eastern Conference champs, the Philadelphia 76ers. The stats of this team are outrageous. Allen Iverson averaged almost 32 points per game; the second-highest scorer was Theo Ratliff at 12.4 points per game. Without AI this team would have never gotten off the ground. In fact, the 76ers could of been the worst offense in history. This kind of entrepreneurship works best for dentists, law firms, or private detectives. These jobs require one highly-skilled and highly-paid leader and other role players to carry out the support work.

The second team is the Highly Talented Cross-Cultural Victors. This team experiences success in so many individual ways it takes a real leader and advisor to bring them to perform well together. Of course, the best analogy in basketball is Gregg Popovich, head coach of the 5 time world champion San Antonio Spurs. In, 2006-2007 with unselfish players including Manu Ginobili and Robert Horry coming off the bench there was no doubt this team had potential. However, the real talent is that they were able to work together despite having practically every race and ethnicity on that team: French, Argentinian, Caribbean, Yugoslavian, Northeast US, Midwest US, West Coast US, Dutch, etc.

The third team is the "Opportunity Seekers". This team sees the value of joining together to create a winning and successful enterprise. Note that it typically is short-lived but often results in a surge of success. Look at Dwayne Wade with the Miami Heat. In the 2009-2010 season, only three other players remained on the roster with the star SG. The remaining 11 were filled with big name purchases staring Chris Bosh, LeBron James and ring-seeking-veterans. The joining of these 3 was for the sole purpose of large market success and championships. Look at your company, can you bring together three superstars for one project? Are you far along enough for that?

The fourth team is the "Functional Teams". Everyone has their fundamental role, and he or she must play it well to achieve success. Teams like the 2014-2015 Atlanta Hawks come to mind or the 2004-2005 Pistons. No true superstars, just a well-balanced team atmosphere. Perhaps you may have an engineer, accountant, marketing, and sales all on the same team... The question is can you function as a unit to take a startup to a profitable company?

The fifth team is the "Dynamic Duo". Stockton-Malone, Kobe-Shaq, MJ-Pippen, Magic-Kareem. A 2-man show, one of the most popular versions of entrepreneurship. These partnerships are not always from childhood friendship but rather formed by sheer luck. Whether being drafted at the same time or fighting the same obstacles in different ways, they seem to understand how to succeed together. Steve Jobs and Steve Wozniak were excellent examples, one marketing, and one engineer that took the idea of a personal computer and turned it into a lifeline for everyone ages 2 to 102.

Challenge

Fantasy Draft your dream team with the partners you'd want. Friends, Family, Teammates, Rivals, Bosses, etc. Make up to 2 of your own teams and rate how great they would be in the industry you're looking at.

Team Name: _____

Partner 1: _____

Role: _____

Partner 2: _____

Role: _____

Partner 3: _____

Role: _____

Partner 4: _____

Role: _____

Partner 5: _____

Role: _____

☆☆☆☆☆

Why would this be a good fit? _____

_____

Challenge

Team Name: _____

Partner 1: _____

Role: _____

Partner 2: _____

Role: _____

Partner 3: _____

Role: _____

Partner 4: _____

Role: _____

Partner 5: _____

Role: _____

☆☆☆☆☆

Why would this be a good fit? _____

_____

Which would be a better fit? _____

_____

_____

Do you foresee fights breaking out amongst the teams or rather a bright chemistry? _____

_____

Chapter 6

Money Management

- "Accumulate assets instead of spending it on jewelry, learn to manage your currency."

One of the saddest things to see is a professional athlete go bankrupt. You know those people who make poor decisions managing their money. By the time they realize they are no longer 21 fresh off a contract, their value is in their fading body, and they never got their college degree.

The answer to money management is to learn the value of the dollar. Instead of spending money on short term investments like a night at a club, buy something for the long term, a book, leather shoes, sports coat, etc. When you begin making money with your business, keep track of the entire process, label income, and expenses. Maintain the expenses with receipts to get a refund when you file your income tax. Make sure you put money back into the business to keep the cash flowing. Accumulate assets.

The B2B Crossover: be smart with your money, only you and a certified public accountant (CPA) or banker should be in charge of such funds. Letting a buddy handle the money without revealing his true intentions will ultimately lead to a disaster.

On a less sad note, the NBA market value is rising, and the sport is becoming popular in the farthest corners of the earth. The value of each team now rivals with teams in the NFL and the Barclays Premiere League in England. Both the Lakers and the Knicks are valued at approximately 2.6 billion dollars. This number is surprising considering how much money they earn, about $100 million for the large franchises and $40 million for the small. It defies typical investment earnings as I'll show next.

There're two money-making ways to begin a business. The first is to build a company that slowly gains loyalty and value over a long period. Companies like Facebook and YouTube, who take it upon themselves not to gouge customers for money, instead keep their customers interested in the product. The second is to build an item for $5 today and sell it for $20 tomorrow such as the Apple earphones. In this way they simply make money and stay in business. Facebook and YouTube have a higher value to earnings ratio because they have not begun exercising their right to charge customers.

The B2B Crossover: Developing a strategy for long term success doesn't mean you'll make money for a while. But if you can hold off milking the customer then you'll get a big pay day.

Business Analytics:

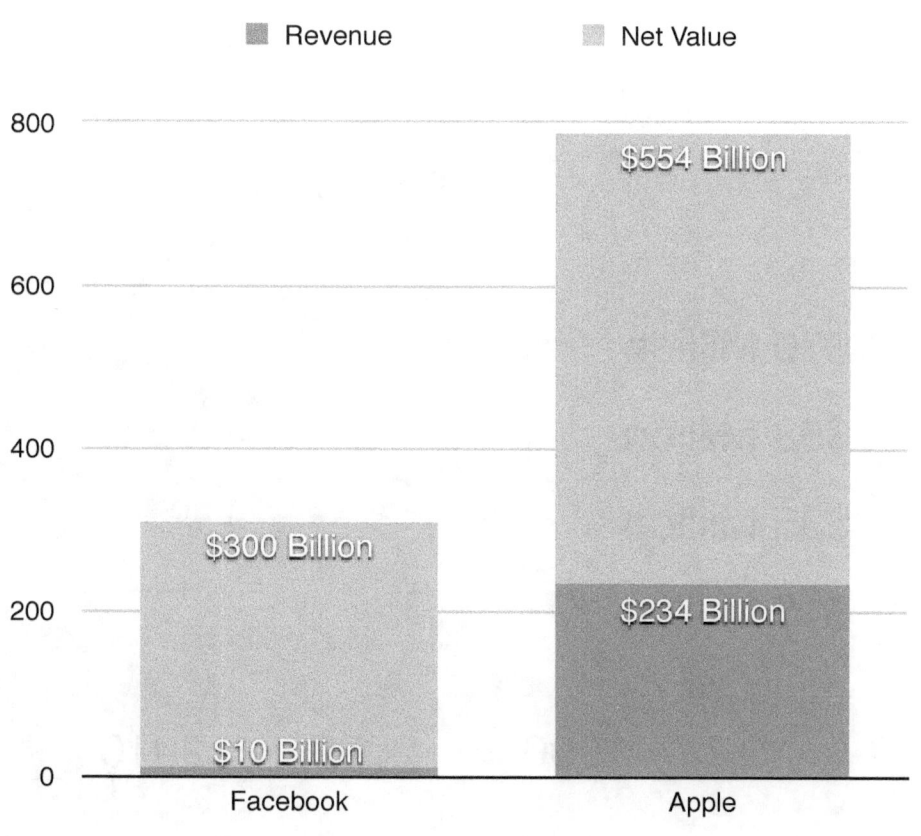

Basketball Statistics:

The NBA Salary Cap keeps rising linearly. Check out the graph for yourself. In 2016 the salary cap is expected to be $89 Million

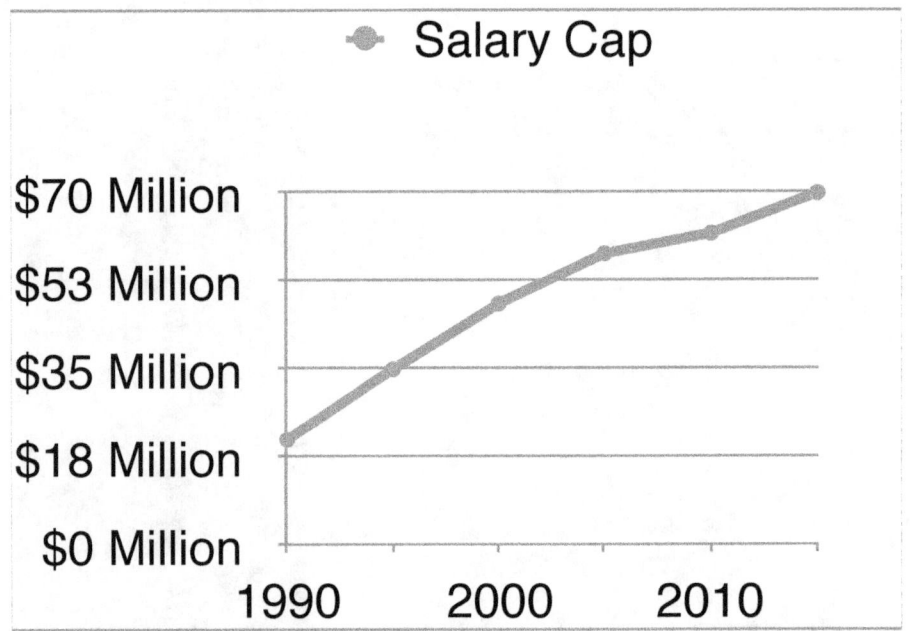

Challenge

If you want to be an entrepreneur, you'll have to live on little to nothing, fill in the check boxes and fill in the blanks to see if you have what it takes to live as an entrepreneur. (1 being least and 10 being most)

How likely are you to cut down expenses on going out to eat, such as steaks and expensive meals? (From 1 - 10) _____

How likely are you to make smart financial decisions? (From 1 - 10) _____

What's your idea of a productive day? Fill in the check box that most applies:

☐ Watching TV (1 point)

☐ Drinking Caffeine and Learning the industry (6 points)

☐ Selling the product, networking daily, interviewing customers, never stopping innovation (10 points)

How much of a priority is being successful to you? (From 1 - 10) Why?

_____

_____

Challenge

Continue filling in the checkboxes and blanks, add them up and see how successful you would be as an entrepreneur.

Can you resist the impulse to spend money online or in shopping malls (From 1 - 10) _____?

How likely are you to avoid spending money on nightlife, bars, and concerts until you've got income? (From 1 - 10) _____

Can you set aside style for longer term satisfaction? (From 1-10) _____

Add up all the numbers

___ + ___ + ___ + ___ + ___ + ___ + ____ = _____

A score of 60 - 70 means you are definitely success material

A score of 50 - 60 means you have the entrepreneurial spirit

A score less than 50 means you have much work to do to make it happen.

Chapter 7

Enjoy Success

- "Finding outlets to enjoy life is important as you gain traction in your business."

When people have a good business thing going, many forget to enjoy the ride while they are on it. Finally, after 19 years Kobe had a farewell tour to enjoy his accomplishments and pass on his advice to others. He is finally giving back to both his the teammates and opponents that have contributed to his competitive nature. "Love this Game" is remember the NBA slogan.

In business when you have a good thing going greed can take over. "Wolf of Wall Street" is a great example. Based upon a true story, Leonardo DiCaprio played a savvy stock broker whose success took him to places he could hardly comprehend. The one most pivotal scene in the movie is when his wife catches him snorting cocaine off a hot blonde's body. A lot can be taken from that, but the point made was greed ended up being his downfall. He lost his family, and later his company and freedom. Jail time was inevitable for money laundering and falsifying tax reports.

The B2B Crossover: Obey the rules of business just as you'd obey the rules of the game. Competition is healthy and ambition is great, but take it too far, and you'll be the one locked in the slammer.

Even the best in basketball take breaks once in a while to re-evaluate their life. While Michael Jordan was at the top of his game, he took a two-year break from the sport to do his own thing. Yet he still came back as the greatest ever.

Say you're an entrepreneur who is very successful making a profit of $20,000 a month. Six months later you may be at about $10,000 a month. You've been enjoying success selling your product but without innovation recently; you'll need to decide to put more resources into the business or consider selling it.

The B2B Crossover: Any time you are enjoying great success whether in business or basketball, recognize the option of taking a break before unveiling the next large innovation. Steve Jobs left Apple in 1984 and returned in 1997 to lead the greatest computer company of our time. That maybe an extreme example, but the principles still hold. (note Jobs started other enterprises in the meantime)

While enjoying success, a coach would say you have got to stay true to the game, and he is probably right. Anytime you feel too comfortable with the game; it seems to spit you back out.

An entrepreneur who gets too comfortable with the business loses the will to innovate. Innovation is what drives success. Never forget that.

The B2B Crossover: Getting too complacent and losing the will to improve your game is a sure way to either sell the company or go bankrupt. Keep on innovating and redesigning products to encourage success.

Business Analytics:

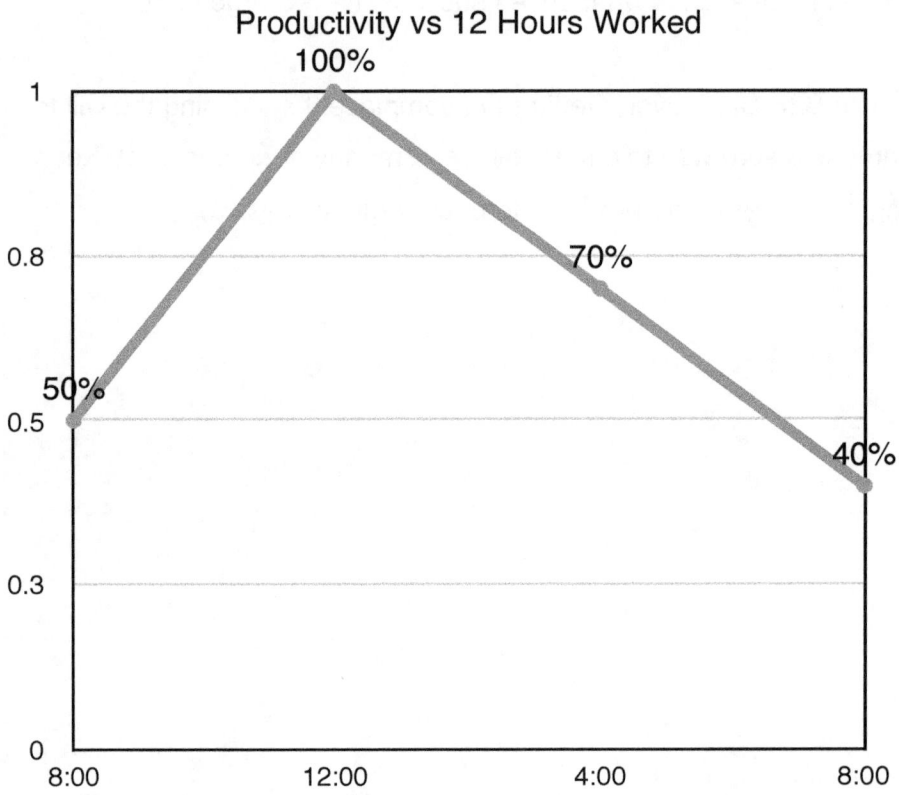

*Percentages based on online poll

Basketball Statistics:

Michael Jordan from 1990-1993.

Year	PPG	RPG	APG
1990	31.5	6.0	5.5
1991	30.1	6.4	6.1
1992	32.6	6.7	5.5

Michael Jordan from 1995-1998 after his taking a break.

Year	PPG	RPG	APG
1994	30.4	6.6	4.3
1995	29.6	5.9	4.3
1996	28.7	5.8	3.5

Challenge

List the times you get stressed out from work that will require you to take a break and enjoy how far you've developed the business.

Take a minute to list a few accomplishments that you've made on your way to starting a business. _____
_____
_____

Now list a few different outlets you have to keep from getting too stressed.
_____
_____
_____

Do you exercise? How often? _____
_____
_____

Do you ever take deep breaths to relax? _____
_____

Do you think Yoga* is for sissies? _____
_____
_____
_____

*Yoga helps people relax, don't judge me!

Chapter 8

Strive for Greatness

- "To build a great company, you need to surround yourself with positive influences, smart people."

After establishing his place in the NBA, Damian Lillard set his eyes on his next task, becoming a rival with Stephen Curry as the best Point Guard of the league. A 51- point outburst on February 19, 2016, against the 48-4 Golden State Warriors proves that he is the real deal. It also proves he has what it takes to become great to put such a whipping on Stephen Curry and the dominate Warriors.

Competition is healthy as the saying goes, which certainly holds true in the world of business. If there were no Microsoft, Apple would have disappeared. If there were no Apple, there wouldn't be a Microsoft. Competition keeps the American dream alive.

The B2B Crossover: Whether teams in the NBA or American businesses. Competition is the driving force for long-term success. The winner in business typically has a similar feel to a champion in basketball. Of course, I do not know what the feeling is after winning a ring, but I do know winning the market is unbelievably awesome.

There are many ways to achieve greatness in the NBA, scoring a whole lotta points, tearing it up on the defensive end, hustle players, and rebounding machines. What makes them great is they were able to hone in on a skill and turn it into expertise. Much like you will need to do in business to be successful.

Challenge

Speculate the competitors on the market locally and nationally. Take this seriously especially if you don't have a natural competitive edge.

Who are your competitors (2-3)? _____

_____

_____

What products or services do they sell? _____

_____

_____

What is each competitor's market share? _____

_____

_____

What are their past strategies? _____

_____

_____

What are each competitor's strengths and weaknesses? _____

_____

_____

_____

_____

Challenge

Fill in the "HOQ" sheet, a common competitive analysis and engineering tool."The House Of Quality" is crucial when designing a product and explaining to an engineer. Below begin filling in the information under what features are required that a customer would want. In an example of a cell phone, this may be the 5 highest priority parts of a cell phone including touch screen, fast speeds, low price etc. Next fill in the requirements of your product, for example 5.1 inch long, multiple colors, 2 GB RAM, etc. Then cross reference the requirements with the features where they line up and prioritize them from 1-5. Then rate the competitors to your product and rate how they satisfy what a customer wants. Their are multiple versions of what goes on at the bottom of these. If you want to learn more research the house of quality concept.

Customer Requirements	Customer Priority	Required Feature	Required Feature	Required Feature	Required Feature	Required Feature	Required Feature	Required Feature	Required Feature	Competitive Analysis				
										Company A	Company B	Company C	Company D	Company E
What a Customer wants														
What a Customer wants														
What a Customer wants														
What a Customer wants														
What a Customer wants														

Business Analytics:

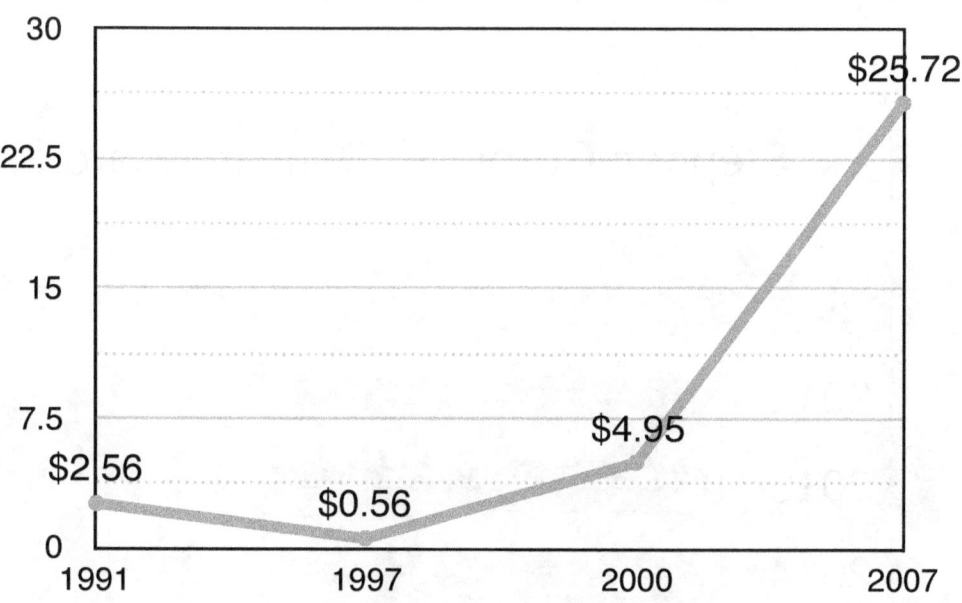

Apple Computer's Stock Price

Basketball Statistics:

Damian Lillard is quietly improving himself to compete with one of the greatest shooters of all time, **Stephen Curry**. It is an amazing rivalry to begin considering as he may be the best PG under the age of 25 in 2016. Here are some comparisons to Lillard and Curry over the past few seasons.

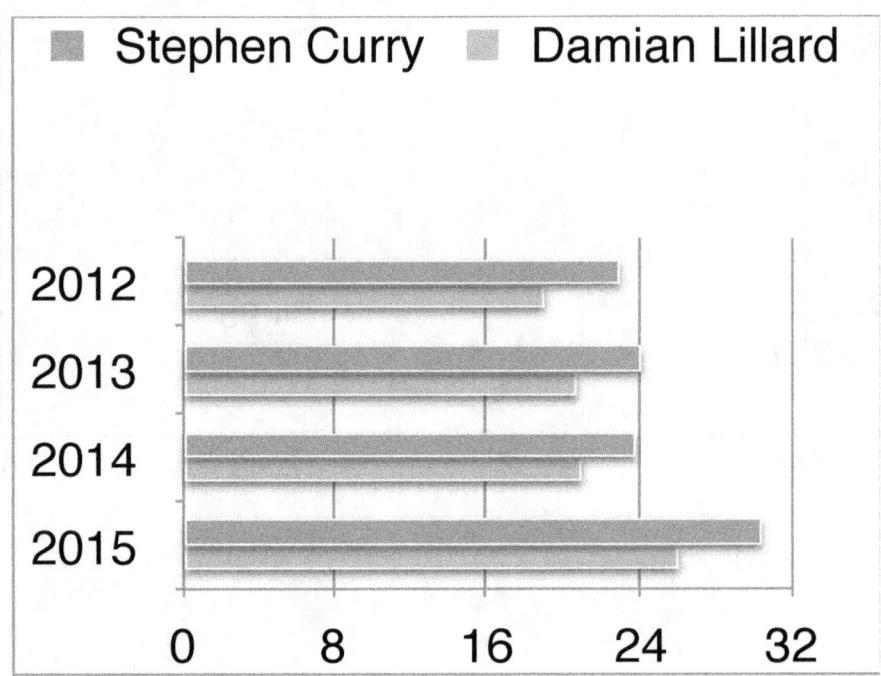

Chapter 9

Bank Shot

- "The bank is always open for business."

Some basketball players are more gifted with the bank shot than others. Players like Tim Duncan and Dwight Howard use the glass effectively. Guards have been known to get the ball high off the glass to knock it in. As well Westbrook is a mid-range bank shot master who has put himself into the MVP range with his ability to score.

In business you want two things-to spend as little as possible and to make as much as possible. However most of the time you have to spend money starting a business initially to make a return income. This concept is hard to handle for many people for the lack of security as it is a risk.

The B2B Crossover: The bank shot takes practice, and practice takes time. The more time you put in, the more bank shots you'll make. Think about business now, the more money you put into your company, the more money you'll make. There isn't a direct correlation because if you spend $10,000 on garbage, you probably won't get $100,000 for better garbage. It's still garbage.

Accidental Bank Shots usually occur at the last second. These kind of shots either are just thrown up in desperation or delivered in anxiety. The only thing that matters after a shake of the head is that you put points on the board, any way you look at it.

Accidental opportunities are everywhere in business. Companies that think of an idea out of thin air, or design something that wasn't meant to go to market. Sometimes just messing around in the garage with tools builds a usable product. Then your friends say that looks really cool, can you make me one? And the rest is history.

The B2B Crossover: whether you spend the entire time making a quality shot at an easy opportunity or whether you spent half a second. If it goes in, it goes in. Success any way you look at it.

Challenge

Determine how much money you will need to be invested in your company and where you can obtain this money.

How much will it cost to make a prototype? _____
_____

How much inventory can you get for $15,000? _____
_____

Miscellaneous costs included, how much of an investment do you think you'll need? List the expenses. _____
_____
_____
_____
_____
_____
_____
_____
_____

How much of your own money are you willing to put into? And will you continue working part/full time to fund it? _____
_____

Challenge

Determine how you could fund your startup via bank, investor, or family/friend. You will need to put your own money into the company to demonstrate to your potential investors you care about the projected business.

Do you have a good relationship with a banker?_____

_____

Do you have a history of making smart decisions with money? _____

_____

Name the people in your life whether it be friends, family or investors that could help you out financially during the startup.

_____

_____

_____

_____

_____

How long willl it take before you can pay them back from cash flow with your business?

_____

_____

If more than 3 years, what are your long term goals?_____

_____

_____

Business Analytics:

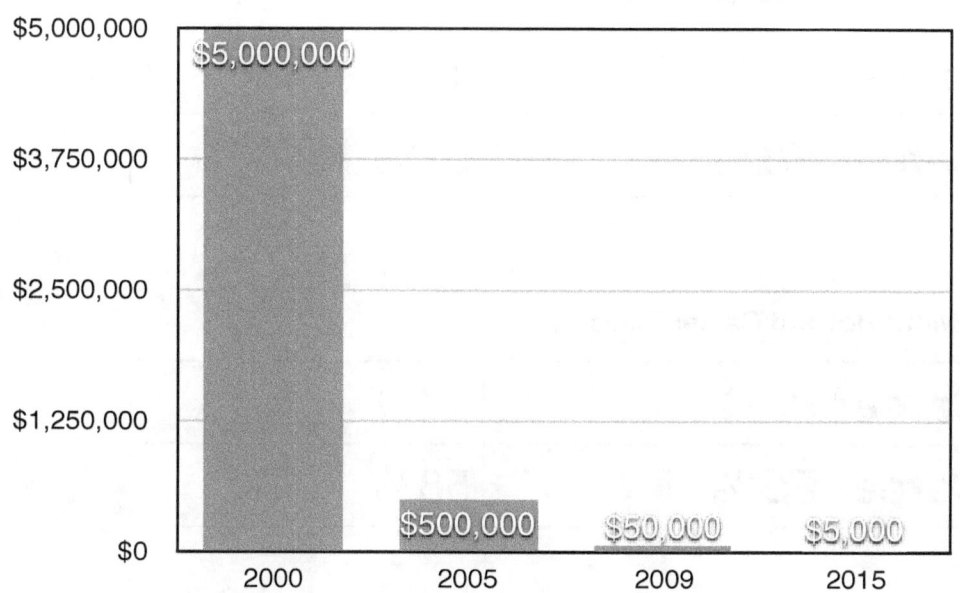

Cost to launch a Tech Startup

Basketball Statistics:

Undisputed these are banks shot pros

PF **Tim Duncan's** Career Statistics.

Career PPG	19.1
Career FG%	51%

C **Dwight Howard** Career Statistics

Career PPG	17.9
Career FG%	58%

PG **Russell Westbrook** Career Statistics

Career PPG	21.5
Career FG%	44%

*All above average at their relative positions.

Chapter 10

Slam Dunk

- "Launching your business will be the slam dunk of the year, sign some autographs."

Get up in the air and finish strong. Don't worry about how hard you fall because with the hardwood you'll always get back up. It really is up to you now. If you want to make it happen, it is up to you and how strong the people around you can support you. You'll be up against both industry titans and small companies. Maintain respect and love for the business and you'll be successful. Now here are the two challenges and a test for your preparation.

Challenge

If you are going to meet with an angel investor, you will need a great business presentation, an emotional story, and convey your willingness and passion towards success. Write down a few points you could pitch in 30 seconds.

_____

_____

_____

_____

_____

_____

Practice with at least 5 friends and family at pitching your idea and write down their responses: _____

_____

_____

_____

_____

_____

_____

_____

_____

Challenge

MAKE IT HAPPEN. Use this road map of an NBA Superstar. Make the parallels to being an Entrepreneur and imagine where your business will take you in 1, 3, 5, ten years.

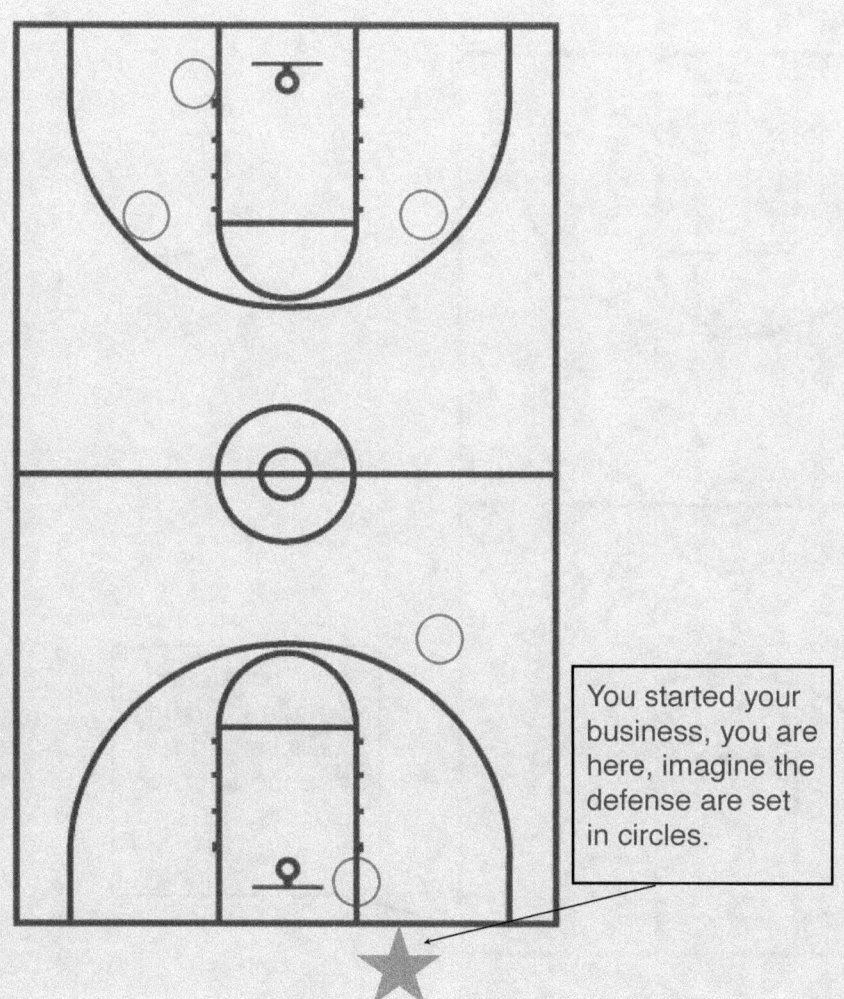

You started your business, you are here, imagine the defense are set in circles.

Test

Correct Answer: Make sure you have teammates. You begin searching for an idea and find partners. Interview people, gauge some interest. Pass to who?

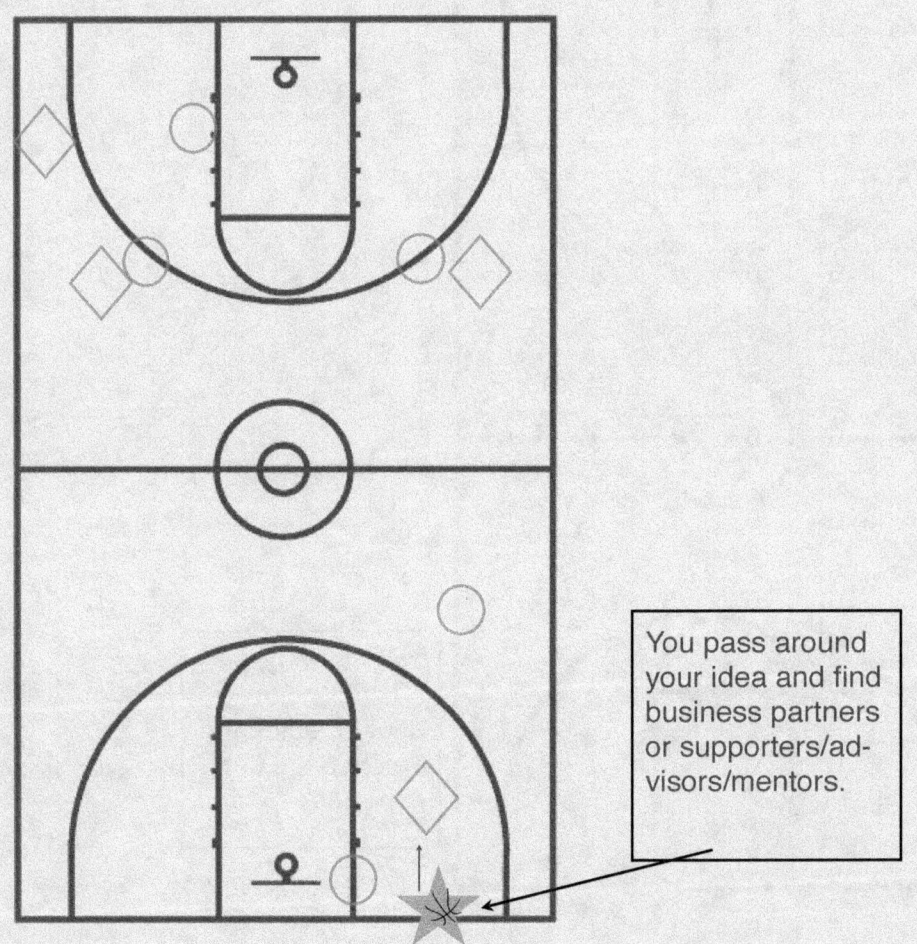

You pass around your idea and find business partners or supporters/advisors/mentors.

Test

Correct Answer: The point gaurd or the guy who wants the ball most gets the pass. You give your partner is the ball; they get trapped at half court. Legal prob lems in business, can't use the name for your company, it's trademarked. What do you do?

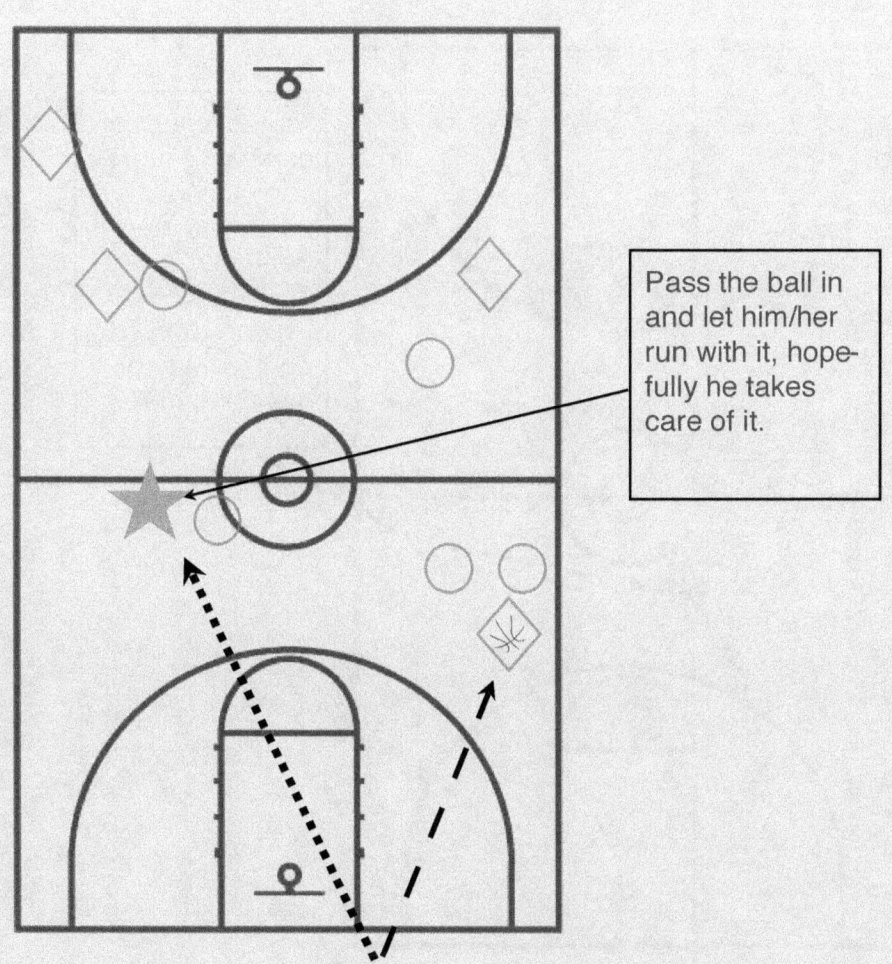

Pass the ball in and let him/her run with it, hope-fully he takes care of it.

Test

Your opponent is back in formation like nothing happened and your team is scared. You've got to put them to ease. How do you make the best of the situation?

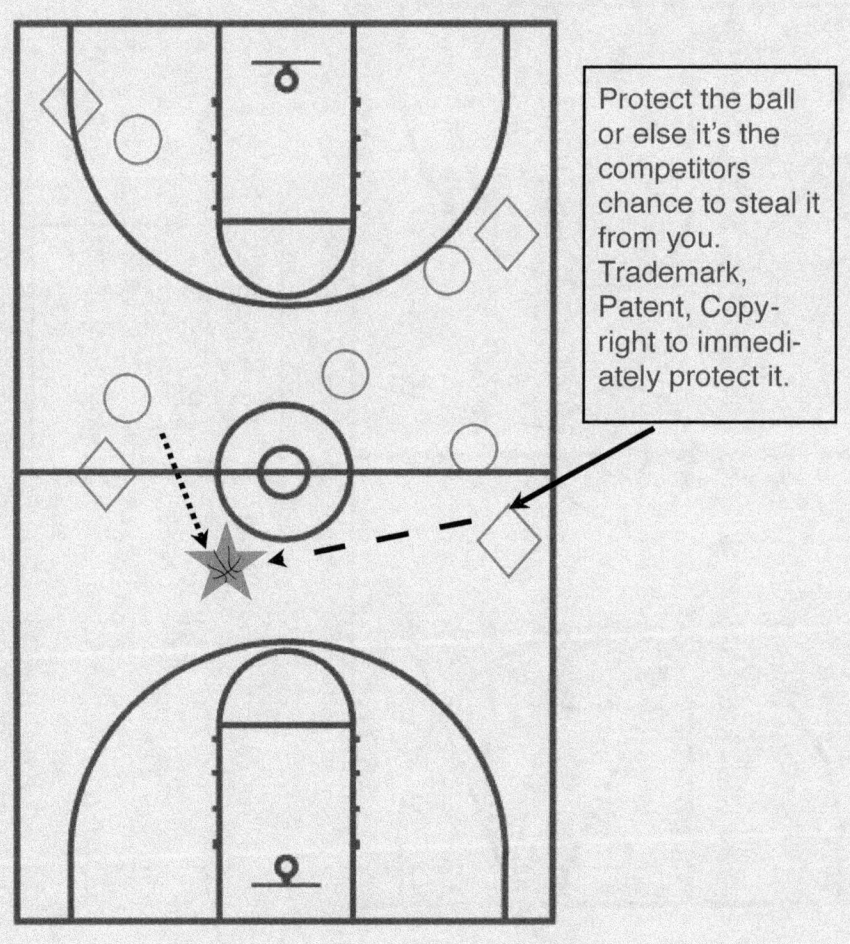

Protect the ball or else it's the competitors chance to steal it from you. Trademark, Patent, Copyright to immediately protect it.

Part 2 Operating your brand new business

Chapter 11

CEO of _____ (your company name here)

"What do rookies and new business owners have in common?"

Think about the rookies when they first sign their contract and have finally achieved their life's goal. For some, that's the end of the line. For others it's the beginning to achieve even greater success as a star in the NBA.

What is the first thing you do when you start your business? Order Business Cards from VistaPrint! Pass them out everywhere, get the word out to the people!

The B2B Crossover: Hype for your new business is necessary for two reasons. The first is if you're not excited about the business why are you even here? The second is that your potential clients and customers will sense your enthusiasm and it will leave them with a good memory.

When people enter the NBA, they are collecting numbers of their teammates, agents, coaches and all of the training team. Staying in the league loop and out of the nightclubs is imperative as a rookie. In the 2015-2016 season D'angelo Russell got himself in hot water by recording a video of Nick Young's conversation with the Lakers staff about cheating on Iggy. It's safe to say his advisors and mentor group just doubled.

Your in business, collect emails and get connected like it's your job. Networking websites like LinkedIn can certainly be applied to your entrepreneurship. However, I would recommend networking in person initially.

The B2B Crossover: Getting connected to people in your industry is essential. If you're an NBA player, the faster you can connect with the league, learn the game, and become a fan favorite, the faster your value will rise. As a businessman in a specific industry you'll have in your contact list of advisors, manufactures, distribution, and other valuable people.

Challenge

Take a trip out to local businesses, entrepreneurial city centers, coffee shops, events, etc. Make a list of all the people who you network with during this business trip, and note their value in the industry be it business advice, financial backing, potential partner, client, etc.

☐ Name: _____ Value: _____
☐ Name: _____ Value: _____
☐ Name: _____ Value: _____
☐ Name: _____ Value: _____
☐ Name: _____ Value: _____
☐ Name: _____ Value: _____
☐ Name: _____ Value: _____
☐ Name: _____ Value: _____
☐ Name: _____ Value: _____
☐ Name: _____ Value: _____
☐ Name: _____ Value: _____
☐ Name: _____ Value: _____
☐ Name: _____ Value: _____
☐ Name: _____ Value: _____
☐ Name: _____ Value: _____

Challenge

Boost your social media profiles by building yourself a brand. People will appreciate your tenacity for adding them and posting interesting business related articles, pictures, advice, etc.

Facebook:

How many friends do you currently have? _____

Being around successful people will have a great effect, add successful friends of friends. How many did you add? _____

LinkedIn:

How many people do you have added on LinkedIn?_____

Add and follow 100+ businessmen around the world in your industry, did you? ___

Post 1 article a day for 3 days that a businessman would take interest in.

Day 1 Article: _____

Day 2 Article: _____

Day 3 Article: _____

Stock Market:

Sign up for a stock market game. That's right time to have some fun, these games give you many thousands of dollars and expect you to increase the amount of money you make. It's a fun way to prepare for the real market as it uses real time prices. SmartStocks is a fun one. :)

Chapter 12 NBA 2K

"If you've ever played NBA 2K on the Xbox, you would know that they track a lot of stats. That's exactly how you will be tracking your business sales and growth."

We've all played NBA 2K16 and if you haven't picked up a copy of it, do so immediately on the Xbox or PS. To reiterate the stats tracking in the video game (I'll pick the Lakers, and my opponent picks the Celtics), the game will provide you tons of information before, during and after the game. The necessities like points, defensive rebounds, offensive rebounds, steals, assists, blocks and turnovers are all tracked among more advanced ones.

When you're operating your business, you've got to track every sale, every inventory purchase and every expense. Not only for tax purposes that will get you refunds but to know exactly how much money you have and how much cash you're going through.

The B2B Crossover: The principles involved in tracking statistics in the video game NBA 2K can easily be applied to the business world. Enjoy the income and watch your expenses.

There are advanced statistics in NBA 2K as well as basic ones. Stats like hot/cold shooting on zones of the court give insight to those who are analytically minded. More progressive ones such as eFG%, turnovers-assists ratio, PER, +/-, and bench points also make a decisive factor in who should win the game.

Advanced statistics in business are not limited so much to sales and expenses but extends to which region is making the most sales. Even deeper, who exactly are the people buying your product or using your service? Your studies will show how well you understand your target markets needs and wants when your product sells (or doesn't). Also, for more advanced statistics in business check out Six Sigma to make your business more efficient.

The B2B Crossover: Advanced statistics aren't for everyone, but they do give plenty of insight into what's going on in your business or game. Statistics have become a huge part of business.

Challenge

Check each statistic that you plan on tracking.

- ☐ Income
- ☐ Expenses
- ☐ Product Sales
- ☐ Manufacturing Costs
- ☐ Distribution Costs
- ☐ Sales by Location/ Individual Customer Sales
- ☐ Money Reinvested into Business
- ☐ Marketing Costs
- ☐ Employee/Freelancer Costs
- ☐ Gas Costs
- ☐ Passive Income
- ☐ Portfolio Income
- ☐ Insurance Costs
- ☐ Travel Expenses
- ☐ Taxes
- ☐ Client Expenses
- ☐ Office Expenses
- ☐ Building Leasing Expenses

Challenge

Who will be on the cover of NBA 2K in the next 10 years?

NBA 2K17 _____

NBA 2K18 _____

NBA 2K19 _____

NBA 2K20 _____

NBA 2K21 _____

NBA 2K22 _____

NBA 2K23 _____

NBA 2K24 _____

NBA 2K25 _____

NBA 2K26 _____

*If you don't know what NBA 2k is, skip this section.

Chapter 13 Dirty Work

"Sometimes you've got to do the dirty work."

The players that are aggressive and in attack mode at all times get the hustle plays. Offensive rebounds, cuts to the basket, and hard effort play saves teams from turnovers and stagnation. Scrappy players like Patrick Beverly and Mathew Dellavedova get to loose balls like crazy, while bigs like Tristan Thompson and Draymond Green play every rebound as an opportunity.

People that hustle in business don't receive praise from any coaches, but they will go the extra distance to prevent a sale from getting away. Many times you'll find yourself in the situation of making a sale, especially a high priced sale, where if you seal the deal you'll make thousands. In these situations, misreading the buyer can be critical, you will lose the deal.

The B2B Crossover: Scrappy guards are extremely efficient at getting the ball and capitalizing on mistakes. In business, you can definitely be scrappy.

Make a sell here and make a sell there. Catch a mistake to turn a quick profit by purchasing low and selling high. In the case of real estate, you've got to prevent an error like that from happening. It's a huge deal to lose a sale of that stature.

Big men in attack mode are a scary sight. I remember Dwight Howard and Shaq in their prime, can you imagine those guys storming toward you down the paint? Reliving point guard nightmares right now, give me a second... On the offensive side they knew exactly what they were going to do, dunk right on you.

Be a big man in business, go headfirst at what you want. Sell your product and make it something people want. When competitors see your product, make sure they clearly know what they're up against. This should be a better product and a better salesman.

The B2B Crossover: Sell it scrappy or sell it big. You've got to know how to sell a product. Learning sales as a trade is a great skill. Sometimes the best thing to do isn't to overcharge a customer, but be a great salesperson for that customers continued return to your store/product/service.

Some great players have unconventional methods to score. Players like James Harden are remarkable masters at harnessing the element of the Euro-Step, the step-back 3 pointer, and the will-not-be-denied attitude to the basket to draw a foul.

Guerrilla marketing is an unusual method to sell a product or service. These marketing campaigns are often defined as an innovative, unconventional, and low-cost marketing technique aimed at obtaining maximum exposure for a product.

The B2B Crossover: While great players develop different methods to play their game, outstanding business strategies often emerge from unusual methods as well. When these techniques are successful, they are called innovative and futuristic.

Challenge

In the spirit of guerrilla marketing, find some unusual methods to promote your product or service. Done right, people will take a second glance of your product and remember it, or they will forget it immediately. Make it memorable and go all out.

What shape is your product? _____

_____

What are some unusual characteristics about your product?

_____

_____

What are some things about your product that people never notice?

_____

_____

Making fun of your product or your customer is a good strategy! (believe it or not) Write down some ways you can make fun of your product or service.

_____

_____

With all these answers in mind, what creative guerrilla marketing campaign have you come up with for your product? _____

_____

_____

_____

_____

_____

Challenge

The location for your guerrilla marketing is all about being in the right place at the right time.

Getting up close and personal with your target market is a huge part of Guerrilla marketing, where can you get in front of your audience?

_____

_____

_____

What time of day would make the most sense for your guerrilla marketing? Example hangover cure beverages would be most suitable in the early morning or late at night at bars or campsites. _____

_____

_____

This unconventional method of selling your product is less about getting sales and more about getting recognition. Try it out, go get people interested with your product or service. If they want to buy it great! If not maybe it'll make their Facebook feed anyway. Write down how it went!

_____

_____

_____

_____

_____

*Guerrilla Marketing has been around since the dawn of time, is gathers massive interest and attention from target customers without being expensive to make.

Chapter 14 The Takeaway

"Take away something from this book and play your game to win the market."

There's no perfect way to play the game yet because the game keeps changing. The fundamentals will always be there, take good shots, create opportunities, rebound well, and don't turn the ball over. However its evolution keeps it exciting. Remember just a few years ago when players actually wore their shorts above their knees?

The takeaway in business is to capitalize on opportunities and make them count. The trends are everywhere; maybe this is your time to take advantage of one or create a new trend altogether.

The B2B Crossover: I want you to think on this before your final test, who capitalized most on the shift to longer shorts in basketball? Have an answer? Really take your time here... The answer was apparel companies like Nike, Adidas and Reebok. The style became something that apparel companies raved about. Shoes were put in the spotlight again despite Michael Jordan's retiring. Wristbands, headbands, and NBA socks were everywhere. These trends are hard to spot and come around only once in a blue moon, but if you see it coming, make it happen!

Challenge

Come up with some ideas of how you plan on making your business the next trend. Will you be innovative and engineer for the future? Or are people missing your product today and when they notice it, it will blow their mind.

Do you believe you have the next trend? _____

_____

When you speak of your product what kind of reaction do you get?

_____

_____

On a scale of 1 to 10 how excited does it make people when you mention the product? _____

_____

On a scale of 1 to 10 how passionate are you about the product or service? How can you become more passionate about it? _____

_____

Interview in detail what friends, potential customers, family and coworkers say about your product. _____

_____

_____

_____

_____

Test

This is up to you, any of the following would do the job. Drive hard to the basket with confidence or use court vision and competitive analysis to determine the next best move.

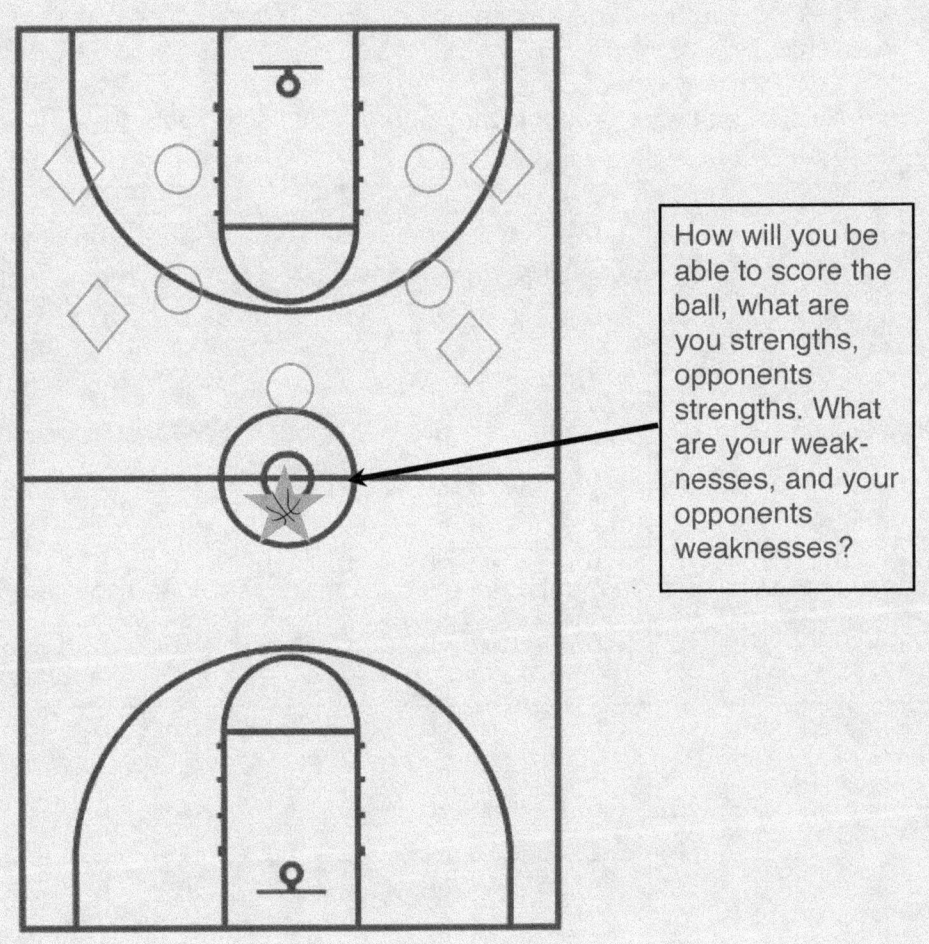

How will you be able to score the ball, what are you strengths, opponents strengths. What are your weaknesses, and your opponents weaknesses?

Test

The first sale is the hardest, get over it, get to the rim and put up your best shot. If you don't have a great product, pivot once or twice or back out all together.

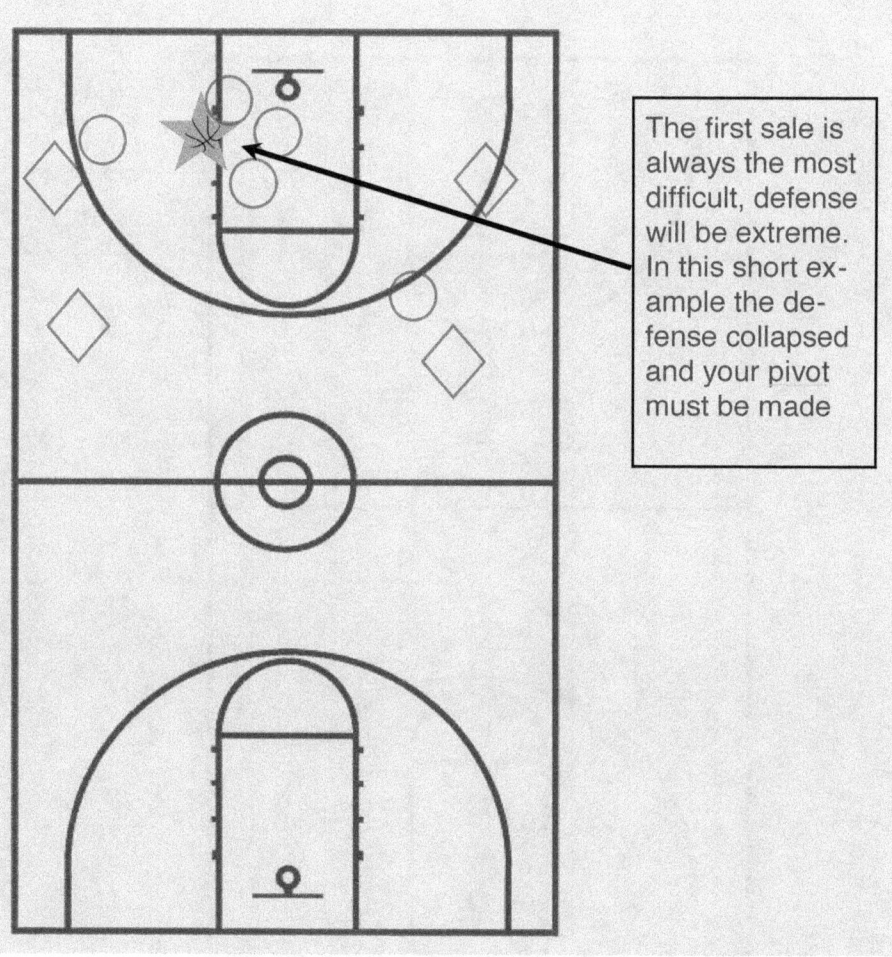

The first sale is always the most difficult, defense will be extreme. In this short example the defense collapsed and your pivot must be made

Test

Never lose sight of the goal and your partners. They will help you succeed in building the dream.

Test

Do whatever it is you gotta do to score your first big league bucket/sale. Remember that 2 points is like the first sale you will get with your business. I hope Basketball and Business are paralleled at this point. Remember to use the all-important pivot in business as you would in basketball. People who are reluctant to change their business direction will dig a bigger bankruptcy hole just like the player who will turn the ball over. Good luck in your Business to Basketball Crossover!!!

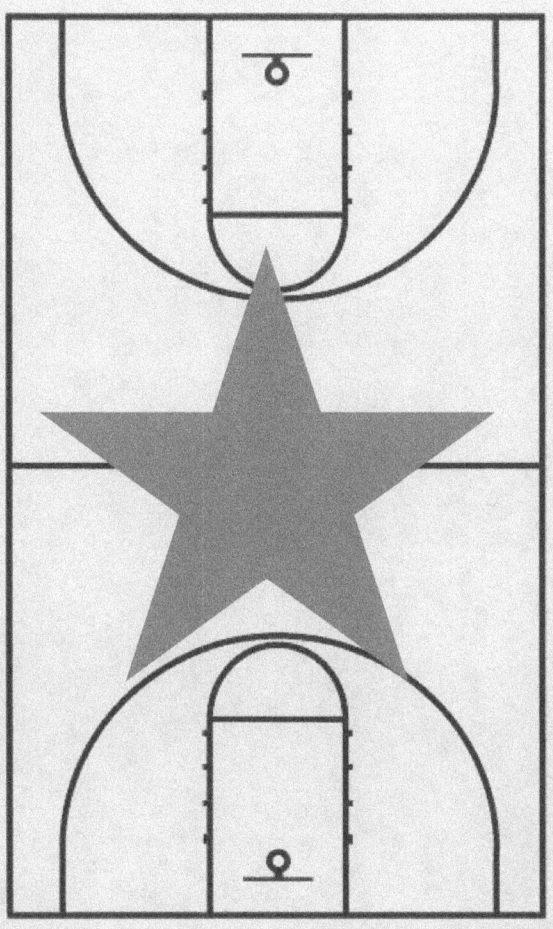

The End of this Book.

The Beginning of your Venture.

Special thanks to my family for supporting me writing this book and through all my entrepreneurial obstacles in my life. My Dad, special thanks for a great editing job and pushing me to become a better man.

Special thanks to the game of basketball and the National Basketball Association. There's an incredible amount of lessons to be learned from the game and it's players.

I use my basketball experience and knowledge during sales, meetings to break the ice. It keeps me goal-oriented and a team player.

If you want to learn more about about starting a business or the ventures I'm working on personally.

Send me an email - cclevine99@yahoo.com